101 Amazing Things to Do in Prague

CW01509056

© 2018 101 Amazing Things

Introduction

So you're going to Prague, huh? You are very very lucky indeed! You are sure in for a treat because Prague is truly one of the most awesome cities on the face of the earth.

It's the mix of historic attractions, stunning scenery, and lots and lots of fun that keeps tourists returning to the capital of the Czech Republic again and again.

In this guide, we'll be giving you the low down on:
- the very best things to shove in your pie hole, from bar snacks like traditional pickled sausages to fancy Michelin star restaurants
- the best shopping so that you can take a little piece of Prague back home with you, whether that's from a riverside flea market or a glass shop that dates back to the 19th century
- incredible festivals, whether you want to get to party hard at an indoor electronic festival or you want to catch some open air theatre in the summer sunshine
- the coolest historical and cultural sights that you simply cannot afford to miss from Prague Castle to the oldest synagogue in all of Europe

- outstanding experiences in nature from racing on a bobsleigh to swimming in Prague's river
- and tonnes more coolness besides!

Let's not waste any more time – here are the 101 most amazing, spectacular, and cool things not to miss in Prague!

1. Watch Street Performers on Old Town Square

The Old Town Square can be thought of as the centre of Prague, and it is certainly the place where new and old meet. You can see many old medieval buildings, but you'll also be captured by throngs of people and lots of activity. On the weekends, you can catch people dressed up in costumes and acting out plays, dancing in the centre of the square, and playing Czech folk music. In other words, it's a fantastic, lively place to be throughout your time in the city.

(Staroměstské nám;
www.prague.eu/qf/cs/ramjet/objekt/mista/183)

2. Sample Some Pickled Cheese

Prague is one of the best places in Europe for delicious bar snacks. In England, you would find pork scratchings, in Madrid you would find Spanish tortilla, and in Prague you will find pickled cheeses. The cheese in question is usually a kind of soft cheese that is somewhat like camembert or brie. The cheese is soaked in oil, vinegar, peppers, and spices for a few days, and then it's served up alongside slices of bread and pints of beer. Delicious.

3. Stroll the Charles Bridge

The Charles Bridge, a bridge that connects both sides of the Vltava river, has to be one of the most stunning bridges in all of the world. It was constructed way back in the middle of the 14th century, and it is lined with thirty Baroque style statues of religious figures. There is little more pleasurable in the city than to simply stroll hand in hand across the bridge with somebody you love while taking in the astounding vista of the city. And perhaps taking a selfie or two while you're at it!

(Karlův most; www.prague.eu/cs/objekt/mista/93/karluv-most)

4. Watch the City Light Up for SIGNAL Light Festival

Prague is without a doubt a beautiful city. But it's during the annual SIGNAL Light Festival in October that the city is illuminated in all of its glory. For four nights of the year, video mapping and light art installations will be projected on to some of the most beautiful and iconic buildings in the city. Places that will be lit up include the Old Town Square, Dancing House, Kampa Museum, and Charles Bridge.

(www.signalfestival.com)

5. Feel Prague's History at Prague Castle

Prague Castle is quite possibly the most iconic and spectacular of all the historic attractions in the city. The castle is thought to date way back to the 9th century, making it more than one thousand years old! Since then, it has grown into one of the largest castle complexes on the face of the planet, with an area of 70,000 square metres. As the castle has been built and updated over a long period of time, it contains many different architectural styles, from Gothic to Renaissance.

(www.hrad.cz)

6. Grab a Bargain at Kolbenova Flea Market

If you have yet to do any souvenir shopping, forget about the touristic shops that will try and sell you branded t-shirts and mugs for far too great of a price, and head to the labyrinthine Kolbenova flea market, which at a size of 50,000 square metres happens to be the largest flea market in all of the Czech Republic. It is a bargain hunter's paradise, and you'll be able to find so many different kinds of items, from vintage clothing to original paintings, from antique furniture to hand crafted jewellery. It takes place every weekend, on Saturday and Sunday mornings.

(U Elektry, 190 00 Praha 9-Vysočany; http://blesitrhy.cz)

7. Chow Down on Pork Knuckle

If you are a meat lover, you have definitely chosen the right destination for your city break, and one of the specialities of the city is pork knuckle or pork knee. This is essentially a huge hunk of meat, and as the meat is all around a big bone, it is extremely flavourful. The meat is even richer than normal because it is usually cooked in dark beer and herbs. It will be served on a wooden board, and served with accompaniments such as horseradish, pickles, bread, and, of course, you should wash it down with lots of local beer.

8. Look to the Skies for Sigmund Freud

Sigmund Freud, the important psychoanalyst, is one of the most famous people, perhaps the most famous to emerge from the Czech Republic. As you stroll around the Old Town, you might just stumble upon the man himself, or at least a statue of him. In fact, there is a rather strange monument of the man hanging from the top of a building. The statue is somewhat disturbing and has prompted phone calls from people believing to it be someone committing suicide.

9. Pay Homage at the John Lennon Wall

One of the coolest and most iconic attractions in the city of Prague has to be the John Lennon Wall, which you can find on Kampa Island in the middle of the river. It was once just a normal wall in the city, but since the 1980s, it has transformed into a place where Beatles fans from the Czech Republic and even around the world make pilgrimage and pay homage to John Lennon and the Beatles. The whole wall is covered with portraits of the man, and graffiti of the band's lyrics.

(Velkopřevorské náměstí, 100 00 Praha 1)

10. Pass Time at a Riverside Farmers' Market

If you're not already head over heels in love with the city of Prague, the Naplavka Farmers' Market by the riverside will take you all the way there. From the market, there is a beautiful view of Prague Castle across the river, and, of course, you can enjoy all the scrummy delicacies that are served up there. For a lazy Saturday morning in Prague's sunshine, you really can't get much better.

(www.farmarsketrziste.cz/naplavka)

11. Get an Education in Communism

After the Second World War, Prague and the Czech Republic existed under a harsh Communist rule that saw 200,000 Czechs shot dead on the spot for trying to cross the border. You can learn more about this important but gruesome time in the country's history at the Communism Museum. The museum has lots of well-preserved propaganda from the period as well as photos and videos that tell the story of the Communist era.

(Na Příkopě 10; http://muzeumkomunismu.cz)

12. Sip on Beers at Czech Beer Festival

When in Prague, it's practically your duty to drink as much beer as you can, and if you make it to the Czech capital for the Czech Beer Festival, you'll be given a helping hand because this is the largest beer festival in the whole of the country, and it lasts for a whopping 17 days. At the festival, you can try more than 120 different beers, both local and foreign brews. And since the venue has a seating capacity of 10,000 people, it is sure to be one hell of a party.

(www.ceskypivnifestival.cz/en)

13. Catch a Fun Puppet Show

While going to a puppet show might not ordinarily be something that you choose to do at home, it really is an exceptional way of exploring some of the local culture, because marionette making is one of the oldest crafts in the country, dating back to centuries ago. The place to catch a riotous puppet show is definitely the National Marionette Theatre. There are stories such as Don Giovanni and the Magic Flute, and they are typically very visual so everyone from small kids to grandmothers will be entranced by the performances.

(Žatecká 98/1, 110 00 Praha-Staré Město; www.mozart.cz)

14. Cruise the Vltava River

As with so many great cities around the world, one of the focal points of Prague is its river – the river Vltava. Rather than just taking in a view of the river from a riverside restaurant, one of the really fun things to do in the city is to take an organised cruise along the waters. As you chug along the river on a steamboat, you will be able to see some of the city's most important sights and attractions, including the National Theatre and Prague Castle.

15. Watch the Witches' Night Parade

There is one day in Prague when things take a slightly spooky turn, and it's not Hallowe'en. Every year on April 30th, the local people celebrate the symbolic end of winter by purging away harmful spirits. The heart of the festivities is a parade of burning witches through the centre of the city. People dress up in costumes, you'll hear traditional gypsy music, and, of course, there will be lots of drinking and merriment as well.

16. Taste Lots of Treats at Prague Food Festival

When visiting a new city for the first time, one of the most exciting things to do is to try all of the local food. But if you are on a tight budget, hopping from restaurant to restaurant for breakfast, lunch, and dinner can really put a dent in the wallet. A great solution is to attend the Prague Food Festival, which takes place across 3 days every May, and completely takes over the extremely picturesque grounds of Prague Castle. Throughout the festival, you will have the opportunity to sample local and foreign delights from more than 40 food producers. Yum! *(www.praguefoodfestival.cz/ home/ ?lng=en)*

17. Listen to Smooth Jazz at JazzDock

Okay, so jazz isn't a traditional form of Czech music, but if you would prefer the sounds of smooth jazz music over the raucous sounds of Czech folk music, there is only one place that you need to know about: JazzDock. This bar is located right on the riverside, and because it is entirely glass fronted, it lets in a lot of light and you can experience the most beautiful views. There are two concerts every night, so this is the place to be if you love live jazz music. *(Janáčkovo nábř. 2, 150 00 Praha 5-Smíchov; www.jazzdock.cz/ en)*

18. Stroll the Mysterious Golden Lane

Prague is one of the most beautiful cities in the world for relaxed afternoon strolls, and one of the most picturesque places you can stroll through is the Golden Lane. This alley is actually situated within the Prague Castle complex, and it was given its name because this was a street where alchemists were said to have lived. Stroll past house #22, and you'll also stumble upon a house where Franz Kafka lived for a couple of years.

19. Party Hard at Cross Club

If you are looking for the very best places to party all night in Prague, you will honestly be spoiled for choice, but one venue that is enduringly popular is Cross Club. This started out as a small local club set up by friends, but it has since expanded so that it covers 3 floors. On any given night, you can catch a different style of music, and sometimes even live music and other performances. But what's always true is that the crowd is totally up for it.
(Plynární 1096/23, 170 00 Praha 7-Holešovice; www.crossclub.cz)

20. Watch the Changing of the Guard

Czech Republic is a country with long standing traditions, and you can witness one of these each day at midday in front of Prague Castle. It's here that you'll find the Castle Guards stationed. These are employed as security for the Republic and the President, and at midday every day there is the formal ceremony of the Changing of the Guard. You will witness a fanfare, a banner exchange, and a tradition that extends backwards in time for centuries.

21. Visit the Infant Jesus of Prague

One of the most iconic attractions in Prague isn't a huge building or an old street, it's actually a small waxwork figure of an infant Jesus. This figure is a Roman Catholic statue that dates back to the 16th century and it's located in the Church of our Lady Victorious. As legend would have it, the small Jesus figure protected Prague from the plague and the Thirty Years' War. As a result, many people visit and pray to the statue for their own protection.

(Karmelitská 9, 118 00 Praha 1; www.pragjesu.cz)

22. Treat Yourself to Oysters at Zdenek's

When you visit a new city, it's important to be a little indulgent and decadent, and what says decadence more than oysters and champagne? If you are partial to a few oysters, head over to Zdenek's Oyster Bar. With fourteen types of oysters on offer from Europe's highest quality producers, this is definitely the place to add a little sophistication to your day. And if oysters make you a little squeamish, we guarantee that their lobster roll will hit all the right spots.

(Malá Štupartská 636/5; www.oysterbar.cz/en/index.html)

23. Climb to the Top of Petrin Hill

Prague is the kind of city where you amble around from museum to museum, and perch in restaurants and bars. While it may not be the most outdoorsy of places, if you want to get active and breathe in some fresh air, one must-do activity is climbing right to the top of Petrin Hill. There are 299 steps to climb, it takes about an hour, and the climb is rather steep, so this is only for people with a certain level of fitness. The view from the observation deck at the top, however, is one hundred percent worth the effort.

(118 00 Praha 1-Malá Strana-Prague 1)

24. Watch Skateboarding in Letna Park

Although Prague is a very cultural and traditional city, it also happens to be very green, and when you need some fresh air, it's a great idea to explore the city's parks. One of the most popular is Letna Park. As you walk around, you might stumble about Stalin Square. This is, against all the odds, one of the skateboarding meccas of the entire world. On any given day, you can see teenagers speeding up ramps, jumping metres into the air, and spinning into all kinds of tricks. It's an awesome sight to behold!

25. Peruse Medieval Art in a Convent

Prague's oldest surviving gothic building, the Convent of St Agnes, is something extraordinarily special. The building dates right back to the 13th century, but today, this is more than just a convent. In fact, on the first floor there is an incredible collection of medieval art that dates from the 13th to the 16th century. The gothic altar paintings are really something to behold. Concerts are sometimes held here as well, so be sure to check out the programme of events.

(U Milosrdných, 110 00 Praha 1-Staré Město; www.ngprague.cz)

26. Try a Traditional Glass of Becherovka

Prague is so good at making beer that this can sometimes overshadow the other local spirits from the Czech Republic, namely becherovka. Becherovka is a spirit that actually originates from Karlovy Vary, and it's made from a selection of several local plants. The flavour is very herbal, and it's not everyone's cup of tea when drank straight, but it can be a great addition to cocktails and mixed drinks. With an alcohol content of over 50%, it's not for the faint hearted.

27. Learn About Local History at the National Museum

Want to learn lots more about the Czech Republic and its past on your trip to Prague? Then you should waste no time and head straight to the National Museum. This museum opened in 1818, and since then it has accumulated a staggering 14 million items from the fields of history, arts, archaeology, librarianship, and music. The medieval collection of jewellery is particularly impressive, with many beautiful items of significant value.

(Václavské nám. 68; www.nm.cz)

28. Immerse Yourself in Classical Music at the Prague Proms

The Czech Republic has a reputation for its world class contribution to classical music, but if you thought that the days of the major composers and big classical concerts were a thing of the past, think again. If you love classical music, you should absolutely make it to Prague for the Prague Proms in June and July. Across the course of about a month, there are traditional promenade concerts that will make you feel as though you have stepped back in time.

(www.pragueproms.cz/en)

29. Take in Some Contemporary Dance

While Prague is best known as a traditional city, you absolutely shouldn't discount Prague as a city that can look to the future. For some really interesting and innovative contemporary dance, be sure to visit Prague in July for the annual New Prague Dance Festival. Dance groups from all over the world are attracted to the festival to perform and compete for prizes. Over 8000 dancers from across the globe have been attracted to the festival so far, so this has to be one of the most exciting dance festivals on the continent.

(www.praguedancefestival.cz/lang/en/home.php)

30. Go on a Retro Treasure Hunt

Prague might be better known as a city where you explore historic buildings rather than spending days shopping, but this is not to say that there is not an exciting shopping scene in the city, particularly if you love retro and antique items. Bric a Brac is a shop just off the Old Town Square where you can find anything and everything from decades gone by: vintage clothes and accessories, used furniture, ornaments, vintage records, and more besides.

(Týnská 627/7, 110 00 Praha-Staré Město)

31. Learn About Czech Beers

If you are a fan of drinking beer, you are 100% in the correct city because the Czech people certainly do take their beer seriously. Nowhere is this more evident than at the Prague Beer Museum. In this museum, you get the best of both worlds – you can learn about the history of beer in Prague, but more importantly, you can sample lots of it as well. In fact, you can sip on 30 types of local beer in a 13th century cellar and eat some traditional bar snacks. *(www.praguebeermuseum.cz/en)*

32. Understand Folk Tradition at Prague Folklore Days

When in Prague, it's a really good idea to get under the skin of the city and the country's traditional cultures, and the Folklore Days, which are hosted in July every year, give you the perfect opportunity to do exactly that. Over the course of a few days, hundreds of folk dance troupes, local gypsy bands, marching troupes, flag bearers, carnival groups and more, are invited to share their talents with the city, and share some of Prague's cultural history at the same time.

(www.praguefestival.cz/folklore)

33. Enjoy the Grape Harvest Festival at Prague Castle

Prague has built a reputation as an incredible city for drinking beer, but many people will not realise that the city also has a wine culture, and this is never more evident than at the Grape Harvest Festival, which takes place in stunning Prague Castle every September. Across the course of the festival, the highlight is, of course, sampling lots and lots of delicious local wines made from Czech vineyards. But there are also plenty of cultural aspects to the festival, such as traditional music and dance shows.

34. Get Festive for Mikulas

Do not be worried about visiting Prague in the winter time. Although it can certainly be on the chilly side, it's also an extremely festive time, and one of the major celebrations is called Mikulas. This celebration marks the beginning of the Christmas period on December 5th. In the afternoon, the figure of St Nicholas, an angel, and a devil parade down the street in order to ask children whether they have been naughty or nice that year.

35. Party at an Indoor Electronic Festival

If you're a party goer, you are probably already aware of Europe's epic festival season during the summer months, during which parks across the continent attract awesome music talent from around the world. But does all of the fun have to stop when the colder months set in? They most certainly do not – at least not in Prague. MAGNETIC Festival is, in fact, the biggest indoor EDM festival in all of Europe, so if you want to party hard, be sure to make it to MAGNETIC in December.

(www.magneticfestival.com)

36. Enjoy a Picnic at Jeleni Prikop

Prague isn't exactly a capital city that is overwhelming with its hustle and bustle, but nevertheless, there might be an occasion when you would like to find a little more peace and a little more green. Jeleni Prikop is just the place. This is actually a gorge situated on the castle grounds. At the foot of the gorge, you can find an artificial cave and a large meadow. This is one of the best places in the city for a spring picnic, so pack some sandwiches and some cans of beer, and enjoy your time in the city's sunshine.

37. Visit the Mechanical Clock in Old Town Prague

While in Prague, you will no doubt spend a lot of time in the charming Old Town Square, and perhaps the most iconic fixture in the square is the astronomical clock. The clock has been in the square for more than 600 years, and it still manages to attract a crowd every hour when the clock puts on one hell of a show. You will see a procession of the Apostles and moving statues as the clock strikes on the hour.

38. Eat Classic Czech Pastries at Café Savoy

There is no shortage of places in the city to sit down for a few moments and have a nice cup of coffee and a pastry, but one of the most special in Prague has to be Café Savoy. As soon as you walk in, the lavish interior will make you realise you are somewhere special, and then when you take a glimpse of the pastries, you'll ascend to the next level of paradise. This is the kind of café that does the classics really well, so undo the top button of your jeans and eat away.

(Vítězná 124/5, 150 00 Praha 5-Malá Strana; http://cafesavoy.ambi.cz/en)

39. Listen to World Music at United Islands of Prague

The United Islands of Prague is an annual festival that celebrates the diversity and immense talent of different kinds of music from around the world. Every June, you are invited to the city islands of Kampa, Strelecky, and Slovansky to listen to everything from Czech Prague to smooth dance, from EDM dance music to inside bands from Latin America – and so much more besides. As day turns to night, the party continues in clubs around the city. *(http://unitedislands.cz/en)*

40. Learn About the Soviet Union in the KGB Museum

The Czech Republic's 20th century history is pretty darn grim, and not least the influence of the KGB in the 1960s. If you want to learn more about the Soviet History in Czech Republic and in other regions, the KGB Museum is the place to go. You will find artefacts such as photographs of Prague in the 1960s taken by a KGB office, concealed pistols, spy cameras, interrogation devices, and more.

(Vlašská 591/13, 118 00 Praha 1-Malá Strana; http://kgbmuseum.com/en)

41. Get Artsy at the National Gallery

If you fancy having a bit of an artsy day, there is one place that should be right at the top of your hit-list – the National Gallery. This gallery contains the largest collection of art work in the country, including many internationally renowned works. As well as works by Czech artists, you can find works from the likes of Van Goh, Rubens, and Renoir. Be sure to check out the spectacular exhibition on Czech Cubism, which gives a wonderful overview of this fascinating genre.

(Staroměstské náměstí 12, 110 15 Staré Měst; www.ngprague.cz/en)

42. Test Your Mental Abilities in the Mind Maze

Escape room games have all of a sudden taken over the world, but this Escape Room has been around in Prague for longer than most. This is a really fun activity if you are travelling to the city with a group of friends. Together, you will be challenged to crack codes and solve puzzles in order to exit the room within your allotted time of one hour. It's sure to be the most thrilling sixty minutes of your trip away!

(Tyršova 9, 120 00 Praha 2; http://mindmaze.cz/en)

43. Enjoy the Easter Market in Old Town Square

Truthfully, there is never a bad time to visit Prague, but if you really want to see the city at its peak, it can be a good idea to visit Prague during the Easter season. The Old Town Square, which is pretty phenomenal at any time of the year, gets taken over by a fun Easter market, which is well worth a visit. Over 90 stalls offer traditional Easter foods, hand-made wooden toys, Easter decorations, and other beautiful crafts. There are also music and dance performances in the square.

44. Stroll the Baroque Backstreets of Mala Strana

There is way more to Prague than the Old Town Square, and one of the most picturesque neighbourhoods is called Mala Strana, otherwise known as the Little Quarter. There are many grand houses here because this is where the elite of Prague used to live, and it makes the perfect location for a picturesque stroll. Amble from café to café, restaurant to restaurant, and simply take in the laid back atmosphere.

45. Chow Down on Pickled Sausages

Prague is an awesome place to go pub hopping, but when you sit down in the atmospheric environs of a 16th century pub, you shouldn't limit yourself to a pint of Czech beer (as delicious as that would be). There are also many traditional bar snacks that you can find across the city's pubs and bars, and one of the most popular is a pickled sausage. These are otherwise known as drowned men. The sausages are pickled in vinegar, herbs, and black pepper, and eaten alongside bread and a hefty glass of beer.

46. Discover Glass Works by Moser

Looking to take back something really special from your visit to Prague? If so, you need to know about Moser. This glassware brand originated in Karlovy Vary in the 19th century, but their flagship store is located in the centre of

Prague. Even if you don't plan on buying anything, it's worth taking a trip to the store to check out the interiors, which are as lavish and opulent as you could possibly imagine.

(Černá Růže, Černá růže, Na Příkopě 853/12; www.moser-glass.com/en)

47. Watch Some Theatre at the Summer Shakespeare Festival

Okay, so Shakespeare may not be the most authentically Czech thing. In fact, it's not Czech at all. But that doesn't mean that the Bard has no influence in the country. Actually, the Prague Shakespeare Company puts on plays all year round and the highlight of their performance year is the Summer Shakespeare Festival. The festival was originally initiated by the famous Czech writer, Vaclav Havel, and now takes place in the courtyard of Burgrave Palace every summer.

(www.shakespeare.cz)

48. Relax in the Gardens of Franciscan Monastery

When you are looking for a little spot of downtime and a patch of green, there are few places better than the gardens of the Franciscan monastery in the New Town. The gardens actually date right back to the 14th century, so having a picnic there is like having a picnic on a patch of history. The gardens were, however, completely renovated in the 1990s and now they are much more visitor friendly with public benches and beautiful rose gardens. *(www.praha.eu/jnp/cz/co_delat_v_praze/parky/frantiskanska_z ahrada/index.html)*

49. Indulge at an Annual Mediterranean Market

Czech food is delicious, and you should eat lots of it while you are in Prague. But it can also be quite heavy, and if you are after something a little lighter you should know about the Mediterranean Market, which takes place every September in the Republic Square. The whole of the Mediterranean is represented so you can eat delicious Spanish tortilla, fresh pasta dishes, Breton crepes, steamed mussels, and, of course, plenty of wine to wash it all down.

50. Get Playful at Sparkys Toy Store

If you happen to be travelling with children, or if you are simply a big child yourself, you need to set some time aside to explore the magical world of Sparkys. This is the largest toy store in the city, set across four floors, that will set off the imagination of any child. Of course, it has all the contemporary video games and hi-tech gadgets, but what makes the store special is its commitment to old fashioned Czech toys as well. You'll be able to find cute marionettes, hand crafted dolls houses, and wooden train sets that would make exceptionally special gifts.

(Havířská 398/2, Staré Město, 110 00 Praha-Staré Město-Praha 1; www.sparkys.cz)

51. Have a Go at Bobsleighing

Are you the kind of person who likes to get active and try out different activities when you go away? If so, you can take a break from hopping from museum to museum, and enjoy a hair raising adventure on Prague's bobsleigh track. This activity is certainly not for the faint hearted. The 1km track will take you up to speeds of 64km per hour, while offering eight loops. Once you have made your descent, you can enjoy dinner at the on-site pizzeria too.

(Prosecká 430/36, 190 00 Praha 9-Vysočany; www.restaurace-bobovka.cz/cs)

52. Enjoy Folk Music at Telc Vacations Festival

Okay, so the town of Telc may not exactly be in Prague itself, but it's less than two hours away, and it is worth the bus journey if only to experience all the festivities of the Telc Vacations Festival. Starting in late July, this is a festival that provides a platform for the very best of the Czech folk scene. The really nice things about this festival is that practically all of the music is outside in the picturesque surroundings of Telc, so you will get to see another beautiful place in the country and get to grips with local folk music at the same time.

53. Visit the Waterfalls of Divoka Sarka Park

While you are in Prague, don't confine your visit to the centre of the city. If you find your way to the northern outskirts of Prague, you will find a place of immense natural beauty – the Divoka Sarka natural reserve. In the park, you will be able to find a series of small waterfalls, and even a mini canyon. In the centre of the park, you can find a public swimming pool, which is a popular getaway spot for locals on the weekend. Bring a picnic, bring your loved ones, and enjoy the beauty and stillness.

54. Find Something Special at Holesovice Market

Holesovice Market, otherwise simply known as Prague market, is the best to go to if you are a bit of shopping fanatic. First of all, there is the food. Local traders will sell fruits, vegetables, meats, fish, cheeses, and bakery items. But visit on the weekend, and you will find that the market also expands to contain things like hand crafted jewellery, wooden toys, antiques, so this market is perfect if you need to do some souvenir shopping and you want to grab a light bite to eat at the same time.

(Bubenské nábř. 306/13, 170 04 Praha 7; www.prazska-trznice.cz)

55. Explore St Vitus Cathedral

When you are walking around Prague, you are likely to notice a rather spectacular building on the skyline from wherever you are. The chances are that you have spotted St Vitus Cathedral, an incredible feat of religious architecture that dates back to the 14th century (although, unbelievably the cathedral wasn't actually completed until the 19th century). This is probably the most important cathedral in the whole country, and it's the place where many Kings and Queens have had their coronation.

(III. nádvoří 48/2, 119 01 Praha 1;
www.katedralasvatehovita.cz/cs)

56. Sip on Absinthe at Absintherie

Absinthe is a potent drink that originates from Switzerland but has become extremely popular in Budapest in recent years. Walk along the streets of the Old Town and you will find whole bars dedicated to the spirit, and one that's worth a visit is called Absintherie. The staff here take absinthe seriously. There is over fifty varieties to choose from, and it is always served in the traditional way with a slotted spoon, an ice cube, and a lick of fire. You can even try absinthe ice cream here.

(Jilská 7, 110 00 Praha-Staré Město; www.absintherie.cz/en)

57. Discover Czech History at a Fortified Medieval Castle

If it's history that you are after, you have certainly come to the right place. Vyserhad is one of the most popular historic attractions within Prague, and it's with good reason. The fort was built in the mid tenth century, and there are some reports that suggest that this fort was actually the centre of what would become the city we know today. As the fortress has been added to over the years, you can find a number of architectural styles from Romanesque to Baroque.

(V Pevnosti 159/5b, 128 00 Praha 2; www.praha-vysehrad.cz)

58. Have a Strong Coffee at Muj Salek Kavy

There is a whole lot of sightseeing to do in Prague, and you might need a decent amount of caffeine in the morning to see you through the day. But when you visit a city for the first time, it can be hard to know where to grab a reliable cup of coffee. Muj Salek Kavy may be somewhat of a tongue twister but it's undoubtedly the place that you need to know about. This is a trendy place that has played a huge part in making the local neighbourhood of Karlin the cool place to be in Prague. But most importantly, the coffee is just really good.

(Křižíkova 386/105, 186 00 Praha 8-Karlín;
www.mujsalekkavy.cz/en)

59. Get Medieval With the Celebration of the Rose

As you walk around the picturesque cobbled streets of Prague's Old Town, it can truly feel as though you have stepped back in time. But if you really want the authentic experience of Prague in not just decades but in centuries gone by, be sure to join in with the festivities of the Celebrations of the Rose. Full disclosure – this festival actually takes place about 2 hours outside of Prague, but it's well worth making the day trip. This is a celebration of the country's Medieval past, with a procession in historical costumes, jousting sessions on horseback, medieval markets, and lots of music and dancing in the streets.

60. Visit Europe's Oldest Active Synagogue

History buffs will have a wonderful time in Prague, and one of the most special historic buildings of them all has to be the Old New Synagogue, unsurprisingly nestled in the heart of the city's Jewish quarter. What makes this synagogue so special? Because it's the oldest surviving synagogue in all of Europe, dating back to the 13th century. *(Maiselova 18, 110 01 Praha 1-Staré Město; www.synagogue.cz)*

61. Catch a Show at Prague Estates Theatre

The Prague Estates Theatre is one of the most iconic stages in the capital city. The theatre was launched in the 18th century with the express purpose of showcasing German dramas and Italian operas. Nowadays, the theatre is still going strong, and it's the place to be if you want to get all dressed up and spend a night at the opera. If you are a classical music fan, you might also like to know that Mozart staged the premiere of Don Giovanni there. *(Železná, 110 00 Praha 1-Staré Město; www.narodni-divadlo.cz/en)*

62. Purchase a Traditional Marionette

One of the traditional crafts of the Czech Republic is marionette making. The puppets are typically hand carved out of wood or plaster and then hand painted to create figures based on devils, witches, wizards, clowns, and other figures from traditional Czech folk tales. You can find marionettes all over the city, but if you want to purchase one that is hand crafted in the local tradition, be sure to visit the Rici Marionette Factory.

(Vratislavova 2/23, 128 00 Praha 2-Vyšehrad; www.marionettes-rici.com/en)

63. Climb to the Top of a TV Tower

The Zizkov TV Tower, an enormous television satellite, may not be the most picturesque structure on the city's skyline. Although you may not want a photograph of the tower itself, you will certainly want to climb to the observation pods where you will have a breath taking vista of the entire capital city. The highest observation room stands tall at a height of 100 metres, and from there you have a panoramic view of all of Prague.

(Mahlerovy sady 1, 130 00 Praha 3; http://towerpark.cz/en)

64. Eat on a Beautiful Terrace at Kavarna Adria

If you visit Prague during the summer months, you no doubt want to soak up as many sunny rays as you possibly can, and that means hunting out the best restaurants, cafes, and bars with terraces and outdoor spaces. Our favourite happens to be Kavarna Adria, which from the outside is a gorgeous Cubist building. Head inside and the staff will ask you if you want to sit on the terrace. Jump at the chance because it is one of the most beautiful and secluded spots in the city. And do not miss the opportunity to try their incredible strudel.

(Národní 40/36, 110 00 Praha 1; http://caffeadria.cz/en)

65. Discover New Czech Artists at Hunt Kastner Artworks

Although Prague might be better known for the Cubist movement at the beginning of the 20th century, this is not to say that there is no contemporary arts scene in the capital city. In fact, it happens to be thriving. One of the places to discover more about young Czech artists and their work is at Hunt Kastner Artworks. This independent gallery is also placing local artwork on a global stage with touring exhibitions around the world.

(Bořivojova 85, 130 00 Praha 3; http://huntkastner.com)

66. Be Bowled Over by a Gothic Fortress

Lying just one hour outside of the city, Karlstejn Castle makes a very doable day trip outside of Prague itself. This incredible feat of gothic architecture dates right back to the 14th century when it was established by Charles IV as a place to keep the crown jewels, holy relics, and other treasures safe and sound. Located on top of a hill with dramatic turrets, this fortress looks like it has been created from the pages of a fairy tale.

(www.hradkarlstejn.cz/cs)

67. Get Scientific at the Kepler Museum

Although Prague is known as an arts and cultural city, you won't be disappointed if you have more of a mathematical brain. The Kepler Museum is a museum dedicated to the famous scientist and mathematician, Johannes Kepler. Although Kepler was German, he spent much of his life, and made many of his discoveries in Prague. Once inside the museum, you can learn about the life of a snowflake, and you can try out a model of a gear pump that was invented by the man himself.

(Karlova 188/4, 110 00 Praha 1-Staré Město;
www.keplerovomuzeum.cz)

68. Have Fun at a Circus Festival

While in Prague, you no doubt want to have some fun and to be entertained. Well, if you coordinate your trip with the August Letni Letna Circus Festival, you could enjoy all the fun of the circus on your trip to Prague. For around two weeks, circus performers are invited from every corner of the world to showcase their skills in things like acrobatics, juggling, sword swallowing, fire eating, and other incredible death defying stunts that you won't want to miss.

(www.letniletna.cz)

69. Try and Escape the Mirror Maze

A walk to the top of Petrin Hill offers many pleasant surprises, and one of these is the Mirror Maze. This is a standalone building on the edge of the hill where you are challenged to find your way through a complex labyrinth of mirrors. This is a fun rainy day activity if you are visiting the city with kids in tow, and don't worry if you don't want to scale the epic hill, because there is a small train that can take you to the top as well.

70. Stroll Around Kampa Island

Prague is a very unique city because inside of the river that runs through the capital, you will find river islands, the largest and most popular of which is called Kampa Island. As you stroll through the quietude of the island, you will stumble upon all sorts of treasures such as the iconic John Lennon wall, the Kampa Museum, a mill, and even vineyards. This is the perfect spot for a romantic and peaceful stroll.

71. Drink at a Former Communist Department Store

There is certainly no shortage of places to grab a bottle of beer in Prague, but one of the most unique and special of them all has to be T-Anker. T-Anker is a must-visit bar in Prague for two reasons. First of all, it is one of few bars in the capital city with a roof terrace, and from this rooftop in the Old Town, you have a spectacular view of the whole city. Secondly, the bar is sat atop a former communist department store, so it's a real part of local history. And with more than 100 beers to choose from, it's pretty much impossible to have a bad time at T-Anker.

(OD Kotva, Kotva, nám. Republiky 656/8, 110 00 Praha 1-Staré Město; www.t-anker.cz)

72. Watch Theatre at Prague Fringe Festival

If you want to catch some theatre in Prague, there are definitely some great options, but normally you are confined to seeing grand shows such as operas and classical music shows. At the end of May and beginning of June, Prague hosts something a little different – the Prague Fringe Festival. It's during this festival that hundreds of performers visit the Czech capital to put on alternative shows, from one-man storytelling shows to circus performances on the street. Make sure you're a part of it. *(www.praguefringe.com)*

73. Tuck Into a Steaming Bowl of Polevka

In the winter months, to say that Prague can be on the chilly side is something of an understatement. But don't be put off by the cold. The city is actually very beautiful in the winter, and there are plenty of local dishes, like polevka, that will warm your bones from the inside out. Polevka is essentially the Czech word for soup. The most popular varieties are onion soup, garlic soup, and leading up to Christmas you will be able to find fish soup as well. The best place for a steaming bowl of thick, creamy onion soup in Prague is Le Café Colonial.

74. Learn About the Composer, Antonin Dvorak

Prague is one of the most incredible cities in the world for classical music. One of the most famous composers to have ever emerged from the city is Antonin Dvorak, whose works received acclaim all over the world in the 19th century. At the Antonin Dvorak Museum, you will find personal objects, photographs, newspaper cuttings, and theatre programmes related to the composer, including one of his violins and pianos.

(Ke Karlovu 462/20, 120 00 Praha 2; www.antonin-dvorak.cz/en/museums)

75. Indulge a Sweet Tooth With Czech Pancakes

Do you have something of a sweet tooth? If so, you might want to skip the course and have a dinner of delicious Czech pancakes. In Prague, you will want to look out for signs that say "Palacinky" as this is the word for the traditional, local pancakes. These are typically filled with sweetened cheese curds and smothered in a creamy vanilla sauce. For an extra boost, you can often find them with a splash of kirsch as well.

76. Take a Swim in the Vltava River

If you visit Prague during the summer months, you may well be tempted by the waters of the Vltava river. Luckily for you, the local government has constructed a riverside beach along the Vltava, which is called Go Zlute Lazne. It's here that you will find people in their swim shorts and bikinis, making the most of the sunshine and the cool waters of the river. The riverside beach also has a nude area, beach volleyball facilities, a climbing wall, a football cage, and an area for table tennis too.

(Podolské nábř. 1184/3, 140 00 Praha 4 - Podolí-Praha 4; www.zlutelazne.cz)

77. Buy Vintage Czech Cinema Posters

Sightseeing can be exhausting. If you are ready to take a break, put your feet up, and watch a great movie, you should look no further than the Svetozor Cinema. This local cinema used to be a cabaret venue, so it has a very charming old-school feel, and after the movie, you can sip on a really high quality beer at the cinema's very own bar. But the highlight has to be the attached shop which sells lots of Czech cinema memorabilia. A vintage Czech film poster would be a highly original keepsake from the city.

(Vodičkova 791/41, 110 00 Praha 1; www.kinosvetozor.cz/en)

78. Learn About the City's Historic Jewish Community

Prague has a long heritage of being home to a Jewish community of people, extending back for centuries. In fact, the oldest operating synagogue can be found in the Czech capital. The Jewish Museum is actually a series of 6 preserved monuments in the Josefov area of the city. Your ticket will grant you access to them all – four synagogues, a ceremonial hall, and the Jewish cemetery.   The graveyard also happens to be Europe's oldest surviving Jewish graveyard.

(U Staré školy 141/1, 110 00 Praha 1-Staré Město; www.jewishmuseum.cz)

79. Drink a Beer at the Oldest Brewery in Prague

For a taste of Prague's past, you can't do much better than a fun evening spent at U Fleku. This pub opened in 1499 as a family business, and it is, in fact, the oldest brewery in all of the city, which is no mean feat for such a beer loving place. But this is no hole in the wall drinking spot. There are actually eight dining halls where you can sample hearty local fare and chug down some great beers. It is also possible to tour the brewery and to organise a guided beer tasting.

(Křemencova 1651/11, 110 00 Praha 1; http://en.ufleku.cz)

80. Splurge at Le Degustation Restaurant

When you visit a stunning European city like Prague, it's important to really grab the opportunity with both hands and treat yourself to experiences you wouldn't ordinarily have – like eating in a Michelin star restaurant, for example. Le Degustation is certainly considered to be one of the best restaurants in Prague, serving up innovative takes on local staples. Order the tasting menu so that you can try a little of everything, and remember to reserve a table well in advance!

(Haštalská 753/18, 110 00 Praha 1-Staré Město;
www.ladegustation.cz/en)

81. Wave a Rainbow Flag For Prague Gay Pride

Central and Eastern Europe does not have a reputation as
an extremely gay friendly part of the world, but out of all
the countries in the region, the Czech Republic is probably
the most open minded of them all, and it does recognise
same sex relationships legally. To celebrate everything the
local LGBT community has achieved, but to push for
further changes, an LGBT Pride event is hosted every
August. There are many fun activities throughout the
Pride week, but the highlight is always a colourful parade
through the main streets of the city.

(www.praguepride.cz/en)

82. Try a Variety of Czech Beers at BeerGeek

Although the capital of Czech Republic certainly has an
epic beer culture, most of the bars and pubs are
dominated by the major breweries. BeerGeek is the
exception to the rule. They actually stock more than 500
kinds of beer, many of which are craft beers from very

small breweries around the country, and from breweries internationally as well. The chicken wings may not be traditional, but they're pretty darn great too.

(Vinohradská 988/62, 130 00 Praha 3-Žižkov; http://beergeek.cz/en)

83. Eat the Best Burger of Your Life at Dish

Yes, when you're in a new city it is definitely a great idea to sample as much of the local food as you can. But let's face it, there are times when you simply want to chow down with a fat and juicy burger. For the best burger in Prague, Dish is the place to go. This is a real local favourite, and the place is no frills with just a few burger options. Although we love the no-nonsense approach, be sure to order the jalapeno coleslaw on the side if you have a penchant for anything spicy.

(Římská 1196/29, 120 00 Praha 2; www.dish.cz)

84. Catch a Concert at MeetFactory

MeetFactory is one of the coolest places in Prague, and that's a guarantee. This multimedia art space supports local artists and all kinds of innovative media. The most recent addition to the space has been a concert hall. The space can fit 1000 people, and they schedule around seventy gigs in a year. Ask any local person about the best place to see up and coming bands from the Czech Republic and the surrounding region, and they will surely tell you to enjoy a night at MeetFactory.

(Ke Sklárně 3213/15, 150 00 Praha 5-Smíchov; www.meetfactory.cz/en)

85. Tour a Nuclear Bunker

A nuclear bunker may not be your first choice of somewhere to while away a pleasant morning in Prague, but if you are at all interested in the country's Cold War history, then this will give you the kind of education that textbooks just can't muster. The ex-Soviet bunker is located five stories underground, and it is now filled up with all kinds of paraphernalia including gas masks, uniforms, and medical kits. If you can't get enough of the place, it transforms into a club at night!

(Malé nám. 11, 110 00 Praha 1-Staré Město; www.prague-nuclear-bunker.com/museum-home-page)

86. Treat Yourself to Kolaches at Simply Good

If you enjoy indulging with sweets and pastries, you need to know about the most traditional of Czech desserts – the kolach. This is essentially a dollop of stewed fruit or jam that is encased by soft pastry dough. You can find these in bakeries and cafes all over city, but our favourite kolaches are sold at Simply Good. They are soft, fruity, and inexpensive to boot.

(146, Sokolovská 146/70, 186 00 Praha; www.simplygood.cz/en)

87. Discover Czech Ceramics at the House of Porcelain

If you want to take home something really special from your trip to Prague, bypass the tacky tourist shops and head to the House of Porcelain instead. Most of the porcelain makers in the country are actually located outside of the capital city, but this is a shop that stocks hand-made ceramics that are produced around the Czech Republic. Classic "blue onion pattern" porcelain is very popular, and makes a great and authentic gift.

(Jugoslávská 567/16, 120 00 Praha 2-Vinohrady; www.dumporcelanu.cz)

88. Sip on Wine at St Wenceslas Vines Festival

Prague is certainly known as a beer city rather than a wine city, but if you prefer to sip on grape over grain, fear not because there are multiple vineyards all over the city, and the largest of these hosts a wine festival every September to celebrate the harvest. The really nice thing about the St Wenceslas Festival is that as well as tasting lots of different wines, you can actually learn how grapes are pressed and discover historic wine tools.

89. Feel Prague's Creativity at Artefakt

Prague is a city full of traditions, but when you want to discover the contemporary creative scene in the city, you can't do much better than heading to Artefakt. This shop is in touch with all of the up and coming designers from around the city, and commissions them to produce original creative items, such as hand crafted jewellery, ceramics, glassware, things for the home, things for the office, and more besides.

90. Get Saucy at the Sex Machines Museum

Love sex? Love gadgets? Errr, then we are pretty sure that you'll be head over heels for the Sex Machines Museum, the only museum in the world that is dedicated to sexual gadgetry. There are more than 200 devices located in the museum, including some items that are dated way back to the 16th century. You'll be able to find shoes worn by ancient Greek prostitutes, iron corsets, dildos from centuries gone by, and lots more kinkiness besides. Leave the kids at home for this one, eh?

(Melantrichova 476/18, 110 00 Praha 1-Staré Město; www.sexmachinesmuseum.com/en_page.html)

91. Be Wowed by a Masterpiece of Cubist Design

The Czech Republic was one of the most important centres for the Cubist art movement in the world at the beginning of the 20th century, and this is evident when you spot the Cubist buildings on the streets of Prague. But there is no building in the Czech Cubist tradition that is quite as captivating as the House of the Black Madonna. The building was designed by Josef Gocar and it places Baroque design inside a Cubist context, so you have the best of both Czech design worlds.

(Ovocný trh 19, 110 00 Praha 1-Staré Město)

92. Enjoy Music With Your Drink at Bajkazyl

Bajkazyl is one of those local gems of Prague that you just wouldn't know about unless a local person took you there. Fortunately, you have us to tell you what's hot! This bar is right on the riverside and it manages the balance of being fun but tranquil at the same time really well. You can also rent bikes here, but the highlight has to be the live music shows that are staged outside by the river on most nights of the week.

(Rašínovo nábř., 128 00 Praha 2; www.bajkazyl.cz)

93. Say Hi to the Animals at Prague Zoo

If you are an animal lover, you probably often the face the dilemma of whether or not you should visit zoos. On the one hand, you want to see the animals, and on the other, you can't always be sure if the animals are looked after adequately or not. Prague Zoo has been open since 1931, and its objectives were not to entertain, but to protect wildlife, advance zoology, and educate the public. Inside the zoo you can find red pandas, the endangered Chinese giant salamanders, Komodo dragons, and brown fur seals.

(U Trojského zámku 3/120, 171 00 Praha 7;
www.zoopraha.cz/en)

94. Allow Your Jaw to Drop at the Klementinum Historic Complex

The Klementinum is a complex of buildings that was built in the mid 13th century, and that makes it the most historic building complex in the city's Old Town. The series of beautiful baroque and rococo halls now mainly play host to the Czech National Library. Some buildings are closed but you are free to walk through the gardens and to tour the baroque library hall, which will surely make your jaw drop all the way to the floor.

(Mariánské nám. 5, 110 00 Praha 1-Staré Město;
www.klementinum.com/index.php/cs)

95. Try Traditional Dumplings at Havelska Koruna

One of the most traditional foods that you can eat in Prague is a dumpling. These dumplings can either be made from bread or from potatoes, but either way they are delicious and wonderfully warming fare for winter days in the city. We are particularly fond of the dumplings at an eatery called Havelska Koruna. This is a great place to try all kinds of local foods, but a big bowl of ghoulash with heaps of traditional dumplings inside is our favourite thing on the menu.

(Havelská 501/23, Staré Město, 110 00 Praha 1 -Staré Město-Praha 1; www.havelska-koruna.cz)

96. Tour the Street Art of the City

In order to understand the arts culture of any city, you can't just restrict yourself to seeing what is exhibited in major galleries and museums. You have to explore the underbelly of the arts culture, and that always exists on the streets. Prague is no exception. The funny thing about Prague's street art is that it's very often a symbol of hope and joyfulness. In order to cover up the drab, grey, uniform buildings, street artists smothered the buildings with colour and life. There are companies that will take you on guided tours of the street art, and this is the best way to hit the most impressive street art hot spots.

97. Drink in a Classic Czech Beer Hall

To have the authentically local experience, you have to drink like one of the locals and with local people. The best way of doing so is by spending an evening at a Czech Beer Hall. These are dotted all over the city, but one of our personal favourites is called Lokal. The hall is large, but it fills up quickly, and on the weekends you might even need a reservation, which is a testament to just how great the beer, food, and atmosphere is. Drink mug after mug of beer, and do try their tartar steak because it is nothing short of exceptional.

(Dlouhá 33, 110 00 Praha 1-Staré Město; http://lokal-dlouha.ambi.cz/en)

98. Get Musical at the Czech Museum of Music

Prague has to be one of the music cities on the face of the planet, and it has produced world famous composers such as Antonin Dvorak, Bohuslav Martinu, and Frantisek Soukup. If you would like to learn more about the country's contribution to the global music scene, head over to the Czech Museum of Music, which contains more than 700,000 artefacts. You will find musical instruments, programmes from historic local music shows, photographs, press clippings, and more besides.

(Karmelitská 388/2, 118 00 Praha 1-Malá Strana)

99. Have a Cocktail Night at Hemingway Bar

While the beers in Prague are undoubtedly of a very high quality, sometimes you just want to sip on a sweet cocktail in a pleasant environment. When that moment comes, you will want to know about Hemingway Bar. This place is a total departure from the raucous bar halls of the city, and instead it models itself on classic Americana with dark wood and stuffed leather seats. But it's the cocktails that are the star of the show. Don't leave before trying their classic Gin Fizz.

(Karoliny Světlé 279/26, 110 00 Praha 1-Staré Město; www.hemingwaybar.cz/bar-prague)

100. Explore the Life of Franz Kafka

Franz Kafka is surely the most famous writer to have come from Prague. His famous works such as The Trial and Metamorphosis are still read by millions of people all around the globe today. At the Franz Kafka Museum, you can explore the relationship between the writer and the city through a series of photographs, letters, period newspapers, and video and sound installations. *(Cihelná 635/2b, 118 00 Praha 1-Malá Strana; www.kafkamuseum.cz/ShowPage.aspx?tabId=-1)*

101. Party Hard at Klub Karlovy Lazne

If you are really serious about clubbing, you will be over the moon to learn that the capital city actually has the largest nightclub in all of Central Europe. With five floors of banging music, there is something for everyone. Just be sure to keep your friends in sight because it's all too easy to get lost while you are dancing up a storm! *(Smetanovo nábř. 198/1, 110 00 Praha 1-Staré Město; www.karlovylazne.cz)*

Before You Go...

Hey you! Thanks so much for reading **101 Amazing Things to Do in Prague**. We really hope that this helps to make your time in Prague the most fun and memorable trip that it can be.

Have a great trip!

Team 101 Amazing Things

Printed in Great Britain
by Amazon